Exam FAU
Foundations in Audit

Pocket Notes

British library cataloguing-in-publication data

A catalogue record for this book is available from the British Library.

Published by:
Kaplan Publishing UK
Unit 2 The Business Centre
Molly Millars Lane
Wokingham
Berkshire
RG41 2QZ

ISBN: 978-1-78740-427-4

© Kaplan Financial Limited, 2019

Printed and bound in Great Britain.

The text in this material and any others made available by any Kaplan Group company does not amount to advice on a particular matter and should not be taken as such. No reliance should be placed on the content as the basis for any investment or other decision or in connection with any advice given to third parties. Please consult your appropriate professional adviser as necessary. Kaplan Publishing Limited and all other Kaplan group companies expressly disclaim all liability to any person in respect of any losses or other claims, whether direct, indirect, incidental, consequential or otherwise arising in relation to the use of such materials.

All rights reserved. No part of this publication may be reproduced, stored in a retrieval system, or transmitted, in any form or by any means, electronic, mechanical, photocopying, recording or otherwise, without the prior written permission of Kaplan Publishing.

Contents

Chapter 1	The rules governing audit	1
Chapter 2	The auditor	9
Chapter 3	The client	19
Chapter 4	Responsibilities	25
Chapter 5	Audit overview	29
Chapter 6	Risk	33
Chapter 7	Materiality	41
Chapter 8	Planning	47
Chapter 9	Systems and controls	59
Chapter 10	Gathering evidence	75
Chapter 11	Audit verification work	89
Chapter 12	Final review	103
Chapter 13	Reporting	113
Index		I.1

Preface

These Pocket Notes contain everything you need to know for the exam, presented in a unique visual way that makes revision easy and effective.

Written by experienced lecturers and authors, these Pocket Notes break down content into manageable chunks to maximise your concentration.

Quality and accuracy are of the utmost importance to us so if you spot an error in any of our products, please send an email to mykaplanreporting@kaplan.com with full details, or follow the link to the feedback form in MyKaplan.

Our Quality Co-ordinator will work with our technical team to verify the error and take action to ensure it is corrected in future

Introduction

In this chapter

- The exam.
- Exam technique.

The exam

The exam is made up of 2 sections. Section A comprises 15 compulsory multiple choice questions of 2 marks each. Section B comprises 8 compulsory questions; questions 1 and 2 are worth 15 marks, questions 3 and 4 are worth 10 marks and questions 5 – 8 are worth 5 marks each.

Read each question carefully and do as you are told. Often a question will have a requirement such as: 'Identify the five components of internal control and explain briefly the meaning of each' (10 marks). The mark allocation ties in with the requirement. You have to identify five components and explain each, so you will earn 5 x 2 = 10 marks, taking no more than 18 minutes to do so.

Be sure to write legibly so that the marker has every opportunity to reward you with marks. Write in short sentences and short paragraphs – the last thing the marker wants to see is long dense paragraphs of hard-to-read handwriting. Don't worry too much about spelling or punctuation: as long as the marker sees that you know what you are writing about, you will be given the marks.

Good luck!

Exam technique

- There are relatively easy marks (as well as difficult ones) in all questions. If you do not attempt a question, you exclude yourself from those easy marks. Therefore, effective time management is essential in order to pass this exam.

- There are always questions which take the format 'State four objectives of…' or 'Describe three matters which…' so learn the bulleted lists of key points as they will be useful in these cases. The examiner has confirmed that marks will be available for rote learning.

- There are always 'mini-case' type questions for you to apply your knowledge:
    - Make your answer relevant to the scenario in the question.
    - On the whole your answer should be based on the lists and theory contained in your study text and summarised in these pocket notes.
    - If you think you have to invent something from 'scratch', you may not have fully understood the question.

- Sometimes there are 'compare and contrast' type questions e.g. external v internal audit, directors' v auditors' responsibilities, etc. For these you usually have to take two lists from these pocket notes and understand the differences between them.

- The examiner has highlighted the following areas as key study areas:
    - audit planning
    - internal control
    - audit risk
    - audit techniques and procedures.

Question practice in these areas is essential in order to pass this exam.

Foundations in Audit

chapter 1

The rules governing audit

In this chapter

- Rule-setting bodies.
- Auditing Standards.
- Ethics.
- The law.

The rules governing audit

Rule-setting bodies

There are three different types of 'rules' governing audits which are set by several different bodies. Which bodies are involved depends on the territory in which the audit is conducted.

The three types of rules are:

- auditing standards e.g. ISAs
- ethical guidance e.g. ACCA's code of ethics and fundamental principles
- the laws of the territory where the audit is conducted e.g. local company legislation.

Auditing standards

International Standards on Auditing (ISAs)

Auditing standards are the rules which the auditor must adhere to when conducting an audit engagement.

Ethics

The need for professional ethics

- Audits enhance the credibility of financial statements.
- Audits must therefore be carried out by people who are themselves credible and reliable.

Sources of guidance on ethics:

- IFAC's code of ethics.
- ACCA's code of ethics.

How do the codes/standards work?

- IFAC's code applies to all audits conducted under ISAs.
- ACCA's code applies to all ACCA members and students working for all ACCA exams (including FIA CAT).

Fortunately both the IFAC and ACCA codes follow identical principles.

The ACCA code

(Remember IFAC's code works in the same way.)

- Conceptual framework – to avoid a rules-based approach which leads to loopholes
- Public interest – remember your responsibility to the public interest and you won't go wrong
- Most stringent – if other ethical rules also apply which have tougher conditions, follow the toughest (this also eliminates loopholes)
- Fundamental principles – see below
- Threats and safeguards – see below

Key Point

Fundamental principles:

- Integrity.
- Objectivity.
- Professional competence and due care.

- Confidentiality.
- Professional behaviour.

As part of 'professional competence', accounting technicians must maintain their technical standards – they must remain up-to-date in technical standards through CPD (which has been compulsory for all ACCA members from Jan 2005).

Auditors must comply with the fundamental principles at all times. Where there are threats to this compliance, the auditor must implement safeguards.

Examples of threats and possible remedies (safeguards) are identified below.

Threats to objectivity and remedies to combat such threats:

- Self-interest – due to financial and business interests, relationships with the client, fee dependence
  - Remedy – be aware of fee dependence thresholds (total fee income from a single client should not exceed 15% of total income of the audit firm or 10% if the client is listed company).
- Self-review – e.g. brand valuations, actuarial services, etc but could include corporate finance, tax, accounts, payroll and IT work
  - Remedy – ensure there are no overlaps between staff on differing engagements for the same client – aka 'use of Chinese walls' to minimise the audit firm's exposure to a perceived lack of independence.
- Advocacy – arguing the client's case and impairing your objectivity e.g. tax work or advice on purchases and sales of businesses or financing
  - Remedy – if independence is compromised, the audit firm should consider refusing or resigning from an engagement.

- Familiarity – long-standing involvement or personal and family relationships
  - Remedy – Identify such relationships at the planning stages to avoid potential conflicts. Note: Legislation typically prohibits use of staff who are partners (e.g. husband or wife) of staff who are employed by the client company.
- Intimidation – include dominant and bullying characters
  - Remedy – consider refusing or resigning from further appointment where such practices exist. Loss of fee income is detrimental to the well being of the audit firm. However, association with a client who carries out such practices, may lead to a tainting of the audit firm's reputation.

Other general safeguards against these threats:

- Safeguards created by the profession, legislation or regulation.
- Supervisory procedures.
- Discuss the issue with higher levels of management within the firm.
- Discuss the issue with those charged with governance of the client.

The rules governing audit

Exam focus

- In light of audit failings on high profile cases such as Enron and WorldCom, professional ethics are quite a hot topic at the moment and are an important part of the context in which auditors operate.
- Learn the fundamental principles, the possible threats to complying with the principles, and safeguards that can be implemented to ensure that the principles are maintained.
- The important point to remember is how any situation would appear to an external third party rather than to the auditor.
- Students must display an understanding of the need for ethical behaviour and its relationship with the fundamental audit principle of objectivity.

The law

The law impacts on the audit in five ways:

- setting out the content and format of financial statements which are subject to audit (these should be familiar to students from earlier studies)
- establishing the requirement for financial statements to be audited – an audit is usually a statutory requirement for listed companies, but is also usually compulsory for organisations in which there is a public interest such as:
    - banks
    - insurance companies (and insurance brokers)
    - trade unions
    - employers associations
- setting who can and cannot act as auditor

- establishing the mechanisms for the appointment and dismissal of auditors
- setting out the responsibilities, rights and duties of auditors.

The rules governing audit

chapter 2

The auditor

In this chapter

- Appointment of auditors.
- The auditor's duties.
- The auditor's rights.
- The audit team.
- Quality control.

Exam focus

The first sections of this chapter deal mainly with legal provisions, so there are a number of bulleted lists which you will need to learn.

Appointment of auditors

Who can be the auditor?

A firm (including a limited company) or person who is:

- a member of a Recognised Supervisory Body (RSB) e.g. ACCA
- allowed by the rules of the RSB to be an auditor.

RSBs have rules and regulations under which they authorise individuals and firms and hold them on a register of authorised firms and individuals.

For example, it is usually necessary to acquire 2 to 3 years' post-qualification experience with a practising firm, before the RSB will issue a practising certificate.

Individuals who are authorised to conduct audit work may be:

- sole practitioners
- partners in a partnership
- members of a limited liability partnership (LLP),
  or
- directors of a company

and are called responsible individuals (RIs).

Who cannot be the auditor?

Local legislation will determine this, but usually persons prohibited from acting as an auditor include those persons who are:

- an officer (director or secretary) of the company
- an employee of the company
- a person who is a partner of or who is in the employment of either of the above.

Excluded by the ethics rules:

Consider:
- business relationships
- personal relationships
- long association with the client
- fee dependency
- non-audit services provided.

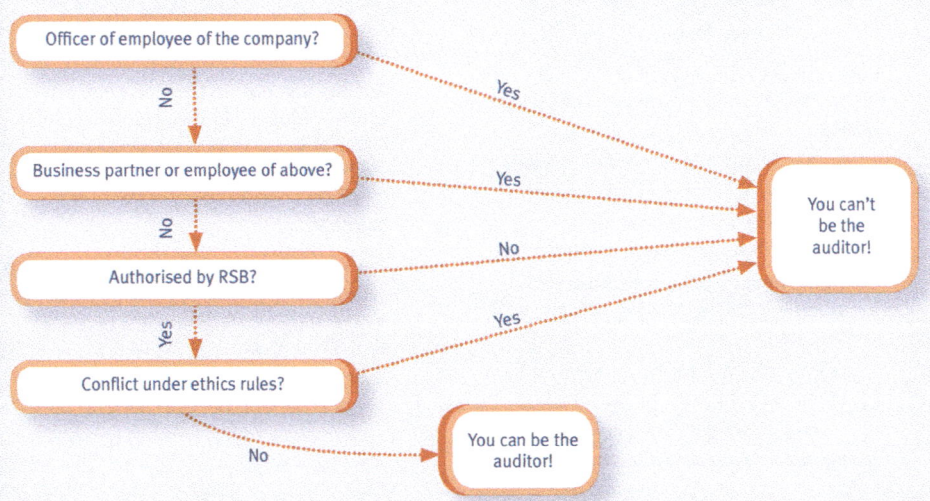

The auditor's duties

Fundamental duties are to:

- form an opinion on the financial statements (this is the auditor's statutory responsibility)
- issue an audit report.

Matters implicit in the audit report and which the auditors therefore have a duty to check are that:

- proper accounting records have been kept
- all necessary information and explanations have been obtained
- the company's financial statements agree with the underlying accounting records
- proper returns have been received from branches not visited by the auditor
- information in the directors' report and other information issued with the financial statements (for example, the chairman's report) is consistent with the financial statements
- other information required by law, if not included in the financial statements, is included in the auditors' report.

Expectations gap

Another example of the kind of information which is required to be included in the financial statements is the directors' acknowledgment that they are responsible for discovering fraud and error in the business.

It is sometimes (wrongly) believed that this is the duty of the auditor. This misconception is known as the 'expectations gap' and is something which requires clarity.

We will see in a later chapter ways in which the auditor can address this problem.

The auditor's rights

> **Key Point**
>
> The auditor has statutory rights provided by the respective legislation in their country.

Typical rights during the audit/continued appointment

- Access to the company's books and records.
- Receive information and explanations necessary for the audit.
- Receive notice of and attend any meeting of members of the company.
- To be heard at such meetings on matters of concern to the auditor.

On resignation

- Request an extraordinary general meeting of the company to explain the circumstances of the resignation.
- Require the company to circulate the notice of circumstances relating to the resignation.

The auditor

Rights and duties		
On appointment	**While in post**	**On cessation**
Consider legal and ethical issues	Form opinion Issue report	Statement of circumstances
Clearance from outgoing auditor	Accounting records Info /explanations Returns from branches All information in Annual Report is consistent with the financial statements Directors' pay and balances	Request EGM Make representations Clearance to new auditor

The audit team

The audit team usually comprises:

- an engagement partner
- audit manager
- audit senior
- additional audit staff
- specialists (where appropriate).

The team structure is dictated by the size and complexity of the audit.

The **engagement partner** is the RI who takes ultimate responsibility for the audit work and who will sign the audit report on behalf of the firm.

Every audit MUST have an engagement partner assigned to it.

The engagement partner:

- will be responsible for top level liaison with the client
- approves the audit plan
- ensures the team is properly briefed
- carries out final review of audit working paper files – the depth and detail will depend on the composition of the rest of the team.

The **audit manager** is usually responsible for allocating staff to the assignment, regular liaison with the client and ensuring the administrative side of the assignment is executed properly:

- inventory counts attended
- bank letters sent
- audit staff are where they are supposed to be, at the correct times
- completion procedures are executed properly
- usually carries out detailed briefing of the team
- agrees the detail of the plan with the audit senior

The auditor

- reviews the working papers – depth of the review will depend on experience of the audit senior and scale of the assignment.

The **audit senior** has to make sure the work actually gets done.

- Allocates work to the rest of the team.
- Supervises the work on a regular basis.
- Responsible for day-to-day liaison with the client.
- Carries out detailed reviews of the rest of the team's working papers.

Note: The roles of audit manager and audit senior are often combined into one for smaller audits.

The **other members of the team** (semi-seniors and juniors depending on experience) often referred to, in practice, as 'fieldwork staff', execute the audit plan, gather evidence and produce working papers – often referred to, in practice, as 'fieldwork'.

Industry and other specialists (including tax) provide specialist advice as required. These specialists can be from the audit firm (internal) or outsourced (external).

Quality control

We will see in a later chapter, the importance of controls in the audit client's place of business. However, it is important for students to recognise the need for effective controls in the audit firm if they are to perform a high quality audit.

The following areas need to be considered by the audit firm to ensure that the firm's own controls are effective:

- Acceptance and continuation of audit engagements (e.g. ensuring all audit staff are competent).
- Resources (e.g. sufficient partners and staff are available to meet audit needs).
- Planning (e.g. ensuring appropriate staff are allocated to each audit assignment for the appropriate length of time).
- Supervision (e.g. ensuring plans are met and problems communicated in a timely manner).
- Review – the engagement partner is responsible for the final review, but managers and seniors should carry out reviews during the course of the fieldwork to ensure no problems are overlooked.

Quality control

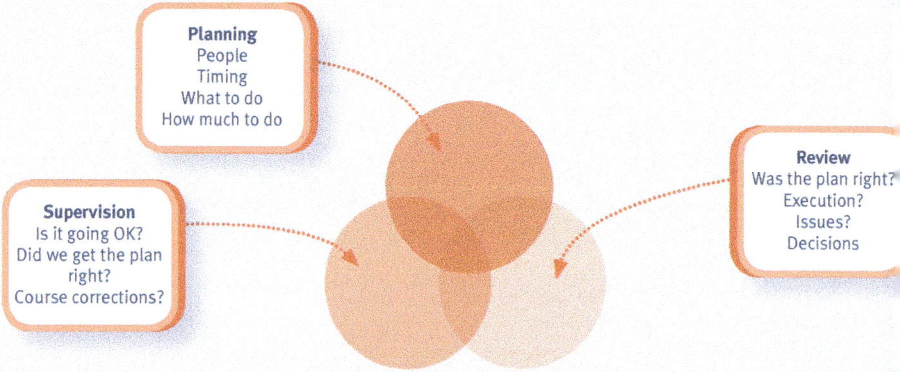

Planning
People
Timing
What to do
How much to do

Supervision
Is it going OK?
Did we get the plan right?
Course corrections?

Review
Was the plan right?
Execution?
Issues?
Decisions

Exam focus

The legal material on rights and duties needs to be learned.

The roles of the audit team and quality control are more intuitive – be ready for 'explain the role of...' or 'compare and contrast' type questions.

chapter

3

The client

In this chapter

- Engagement considerations.
- The engagement process.
- Dealing with the client.

The client

Engagement considerations

The following factors need to be taken into consideration prior to formalising an auditor-client relationship;

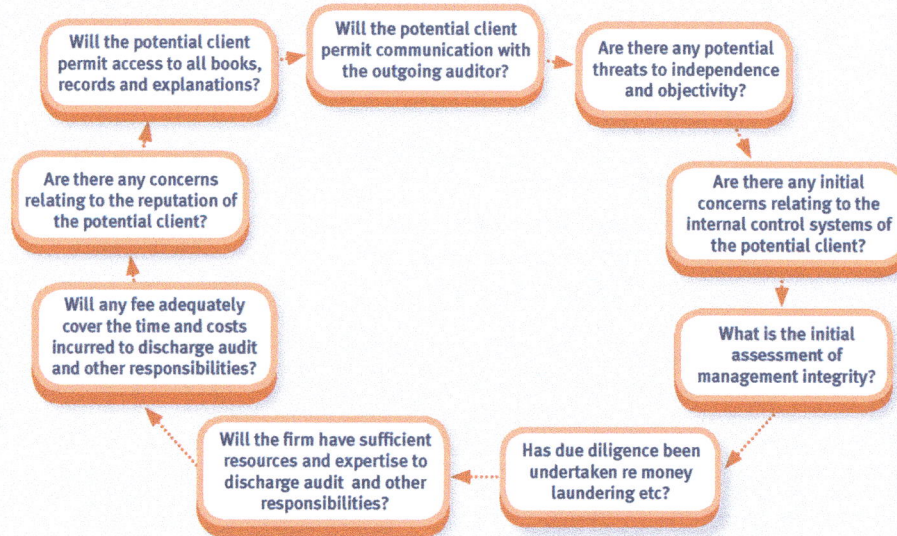

The engagement process

The diagram represents an overview of the engagement process, which is formalised by the issue of an engagement letter.

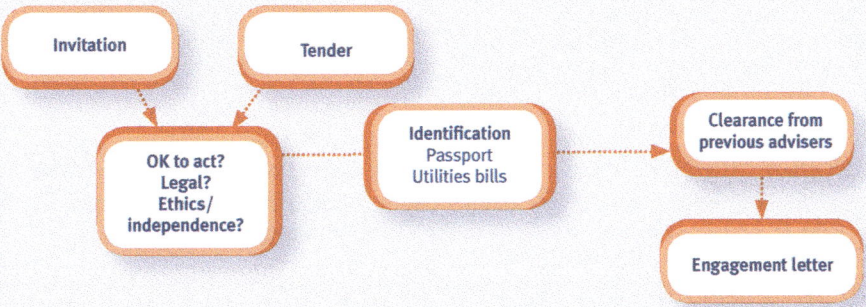

The audit firm may be invited by the directors of a company to become their auditor, or may be invited to take part in a tendering process alongside other firms.

Once the firm has been invited, and has decided that there are no legal or ethical impediments to appointment, the firm must:

- follow the rules of anti-money laundering regulations to ensure that the business is legitimate (e.g. confirm the identity of senior management by inspecting their passport)

The client

- contact the outgoing auditor (as previously described) to confirm there are no reasons why the appointment should not be accepted.

The engagement letter contains the contractual terms between the auditor and the client and ISA 210 provides guidance on what the contents of the letter should cover:

- objective of the audit
- management's responsibility
- scope of the audit
- form of reports and other communications
- audit limitations
- the auditor's right of access.

May include:

- arrangements about planning and performance of the audit
- management representations
- confirmation of terms
- other reports/letters
- confidentiality arrangements
- basis for fees (note: this does not include the quantification of the fee, just the basis – e.g. an hourly rate will be charged for the number of hours spent on the audit).

Professional bodies normally suggest that the letter should:

- clarify the auditor's responsibilities
- outline procedures if there are disagreements or complaints.

Exam focus

In an earlier chapter, the matter of the 'expectations gap' was introduced. Students should recognise that the engagement letter is an ideal and timely opportunity to remove manage the gap, by clarifying the respective roles of auditor and client, so that problems do not arise in the later stages of the audit process.

Dealing with the client

Earlier in these notes, we stated that it is the shareholders who are responsible for appointing and removing the auditor. However, it is important for students to recognise that, in practice, audit dealings will usually be carried out with the directors and employees of the business.

Key Point

The ACCA code of ethics includes professional behaviour as a fundamental principle. We must act with courtesy and consideration when conducting an audit assignment.

Potential areas for conflict

- The auditor has rights of access.
- The auditor has the right to explanations and answers to questions.

but

- The client pays the fee.
- Information is more easily obtained where there is a good working relationship.

Also there is a need to maintain:

- independence
- objectivity
- professional scepticism.

Exam focus

You will need to remember the lists presented here and also think about and explain client relationships.

The client

chapter 4

Responsibilities

In this chapter

- Auditor's responsibilities.
- Management's responsibilities.
- Internal v external audit.
- Fraud and error.

Responsibilities

Auditor's responsibilities

The auditor's main statutory responsibility is the forming of an independent opinion on the 'true and fair' view of the financial statements, based on sufficient appropriate evidence.

Meaning of 'true and fair'

There is no absolute definition of this term, yet it is a key principle in the undertakings of the auditor.

Therefore, the financial statements are said to represent a 'true and fair' view when they are:

- compliant with applicable accounting standards and practices
- compliant with applicable law and regulations
- prepared so as not to be misleading
- prepared on a consistent basis.

Management's responsibilities

- Safeguarding assets.
- Maintaining books and records.
- Preparation and delivery of financial statements.
- Internal control systems.
- Fraud prevention.
- Compliance with laws and regulations.

Internal v external audit

Internal audit (ISA 610)

- Determined by management.
- Accountable to management.
- Appointment / dismissal controlled by management.
- No qualification necessary.
- Role to ensure existence of effective controls and an efficient accounting system in the organisation, providing accurate management information.
- Liaise with the external auditor to facilitate an efficient external audit.

External audit

- Determined by statute.
- Accountable to shareholders.
- Appointment / dismissal controlled by shareholders.
- Must be independent and registered with an RSB.
- Role to arrive at opinion for the shareholders regarding the true and fair view presented by the financial statements.

Fraud and error

Firstly, students must demonstrate an understanding of the difference between fraud (ISA 240) and error.

Generally, the difference is one of intention. If someone intends to mislead or misrepresent, it is considered to be fraud. However, if there is unintentional misleading or misrepresentation, it is considered to be an error.

Next we must consider the roles of the auditor and management in terms of fraud and error.

Management is responsible for:
- preventing fraud
- detecting fraud.

External auditors are not responsible for:
- preventing fraud
- detecting fraud.

The misunderstanding of the roles was highlighted earlier, when we learnt about the 'expectations gap'. However, professional practice requires that the auditor should plan and perform the audit so as to have a reasonable expectation of discovering material error or misstatement in the financial statements, however it may occur.

Exam focus

You need a clear idea of the differences between the roles of management, internal audit and external audit, for 'explain/compare and contrast' type questions.

chapter

5

Audit overview

In this chapter

- Reason for the audit.
- Objective of the audit.
- Reasonable assurance.
- Risk.
- Stages of the audit.

Words to understand

Reason for the audit

The main reasons why an external audit is necessary:

- The directors / managers of the organisation are accountable to the shareholders, who are usually not involved in the day-to-day running of the organisation. Therefore, need an independent check to ensure that the financial reports represent an accurate depiction of the state of affairs of the organisation.
- Listed companies and some other organisations (e.g. Insurance companies and banks) are also usually required to be subjected to an independent audit by local statute.

Main advantages and disadvantages of an audit

Advantages

- Shareholders satisfied that their interest in the company is being reported accurately.
- Disputes settled more readily.
- Can be used to assist in identifying areas of business requiring improvement.
- Loan / finance applications are facilitated
- Major changes (such as change in shareholder / investor) are more easily accommodated.

Disadvantages

- Audit does not guarantee the discovery of fraud or error.
- Considerable expense to business.
- Time consuming for staff and management.

Objective of the audit

Definition

The objective of an audit of financial statements is to enable the auditor to express an opinion whether the financial statements are prepared, in all material respects, in accordance with an applicable financial reporting framework.

The phrases used to express the auditor's opinion are 'give a true and fair view' or 'present fairly in all material respects' which are equivalent terms.

ISA 200 identifies the objective of an audit as being: 'to enable the auditor to express an opinion whether the financial statements are prepared, in all material respects, in accordance with an identified financial reporting framework'.

Reasonable assurance

Definition

Reasonable assurance = high level of assurance, but not absolute.

Not absolute assurance because of:

- testing (the methodology used is not guaranteed to be fool-proof)
- limitations of internal controls (despite the presence of controls, things can still go wrong)
- evidence is persuasive rather than conclusive
- impracticality of examining all items in a population (the auditor usually tests a sample of items rather than everything)
- possibility of collusion or fraud.

Risk

Key Point

The auditor should plan and perform the audit to reduce audit risk to an acceptably low level that is consistent with the objective of an audit.

[ISA 200]

We will look at, and consider in more detail, the area of 'risk' in the next chapter.

Stages of the audit

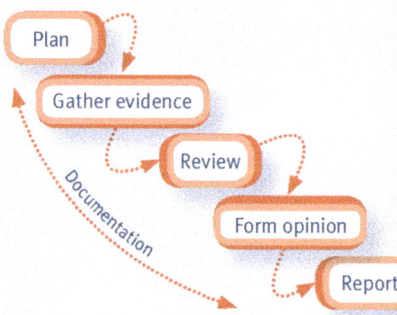

Exam focus

Key concepts:

- the audit report as the objective of the audit
- reasonable not absolute assurance
- the objective of audit work is to reduce audit risk.

chapter 6

Risk

In this chapter

- The importance of risk.
- Audit risk.

The importance of risk

The level of risk at an audit client determines:

- the nature of audit procedures, and
- the extent of audit procedures.

The impact of ISAs

Since the introduction of ISAs (especially: the 'risk ISAs' of:

- ISA 315 Identifying and assessing the risks of material misstatement through understanding the entity and its environment
- ISA 330 The auditor's responses to assessed risks

all audits are now risk-based audits.

Audit risk

What is audit risk?

Definition

Audit risk is the risk that the auditor arrives at an inappropriate decision regarding the true and fair view of the financial statements.

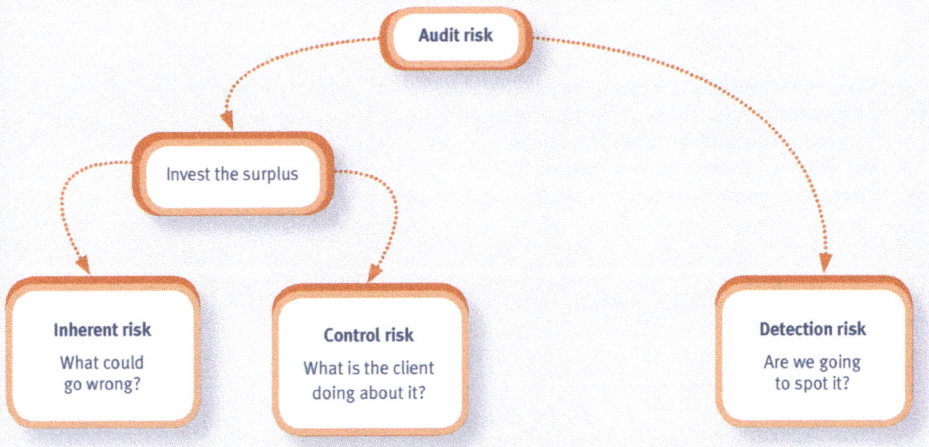

Risk

Audit risk is made up of 3 components:

CR = control risk

IR = inherent risk

DR = detection risk

Inherent risk

Definition

Inherent risk is the susceptibility of an assertion to a misstatement that could be material, individually or when aggregated with other misstatements assuming that there were no related internal controls.

Impact of inherent risk could be at:

- industry/environment level
- entity (client company) level
- account or balance level
- assertion level.

At industry/environment level, consider:

- economic factors e.g. boom/recession, etc
- nature of industry:
  - high tech
  - trendy
  - cut-throat competition
  - highly regulated
  - volatile market, etc.

Chapter 6

At entity level, consider:

- nature of business
- financial situation of entity:
  - loss maker
  - cash flow/going concern problems
  - declining revenue
  - increasing competition
  - shrinking markets
  - contemplating merger/acquisition
  - contemplating sale/break up
- competence/commitment of management / staff
  - ethics
  - training
  - motivation
  - morale
- integrity of management/staff
  - are they unethical?
  - are they under financial pressure?

At account or balance level, consider:

- nature of balance, especially assets e.g. cash or attractive portable inventory or non-current assets compared with heavy machinery or low value inventory
- degree of estimation involved:
  - irrecoverable receivables
  - impairment of non-current assets
  - warranty provisions
  - development expenditure.

At assertion level, consider likelihood of:

- overstatement
- understatement
- allocation/classification difficulties
- cut-off problems.

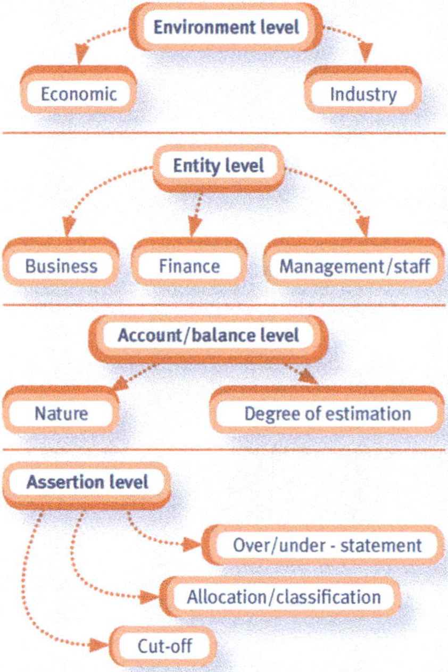

Risk

- Environment level
  - Economic
  - Industry
- Entity level
  - Business
  - Finance
  - Management/staff
- Account/balance level
  - Nature
  - Degree of estimation
- Assertion level
  - Over/under - statement
  - Allocation/classification
  - Cut-off

Control risk

Definition

Control risk is the risk that a misstatement that could occur in an assertion and that could be material, individually or when aggregated with other misstatements, will not be prevented or detected and corrected on a timely basis by the entity's internal control.

Key Point

- Good controls = low control risk.
- Bad controls = high control risk.

Chapter 6

Detection risk

Definition

Detection risk is the risk that the auditor's procedures will not detect a misstatement that exists in an assertion that could be material, individually or when aggregated with other misstatements.

The higher the level of risk, the more work has to be done for the same level of materiality.

However increasing the extent of an audit procedure is effective only if the audit procedure is relevant to the specific risk.

So simply increasing the sample size or ticking more invoices is not necessarily enough – the work has to deliver a reduced level of risk.

Exam focus

- Understand that the level of risk drives the audit work. For any questions asking for suitable procedures you will need to consider the risk implications.
- Remember and understand the difference between the three components of audit risk:
  - Inherent risk – What could go wrong?
  - Control risk – What is the client doing about it?
  - Detection risk – How likely are we to spot it?

Students must be familiar with the definitions for AR, CR, IR and DR.

Students should be able to recognise and understand, through this worked example, the importance of the relationship between the functions of AR.

Risk

So, for example, if NALPAK Company were to improve its internal control systems (ICS), then the AR will be reduced.

Another impact of an improvement in the company's ICS is that DR can be increased. Therefore, the auditor may be able to reduce the amount of audit testing carried out.

Each audit assignment will carry its own elements of risk. The issue for the auditor is one of ensuring the audit is managed so that the level of risk involved is acceptable.

chapter 7

Materiality

In this chapter

- What is materiality?
- Why is materiality important?
- What is tolerable misstatement?

Materiality

What is materiality?

Materiality is one of the fundamental principles which underpin the audit process.

We saw in an earlier chapter how the auditor does not test 100% of the transactions of the business, as this would be impractical.

Knowing what areas of the business to test involves professional judgement on behalf of the auditor, which is usually based on the most material areas of the business.

Definition

Misstatements, including omissions, are considered to be material if they, individually or in the aggregate, could reasonably be expected to influence the economic decisions of users taken on the basis of the financial statements.

[ISA 320]

Materiality is:

- a big amount of money (material by value)
- an amount which, although not big:
  - triggers a threshold. For example, turns a profit into a loss, or vice versa, or
  - indicates future developments or other significant events. For example, changes in legislation (which could affect licences, future trading, etc), or
  - whose disclosure is compulsory (material by nature). For example, disclosure of a director's loan, or related party transactions.

Key Point

A number of immaterial errors could together add up to a material misstatement.

Definition

Performance materiality refers to the amount set by the auditor at **less** than materiality for the financial statements as a whole to reduce to an appropriately low level the probability that the aggregate of uncorrected and undetected misstatements exceeds materiality for the financial statements as a whole.

Example

An investor wants to buy the total share capital of Fun Company for $20m.

The initial review of the FS revealed that net assets = $20m.

However, after a detailed review, the following errors were identified.

1. Receivables = $3m was double counted
2. Payables = $0.2m was omitted

Required:

Comment on the likely materiality of both.

Answer:

1. You should have calculated that the overstatement of the Receivable resulted in an overstatement of the net worth of the company by approx. 15%.

Materiality

> Would the investor change their mind? The answer is likely to be 'yes'. Therefore, the error in the Receivable is a material one for the investor in making a decision on whether to invest.
>
> 2. You should have calculated that the understatement of the Payable resulted in an overstatement of the net worth of the company by approx. 1%.
>
>   Would the investor change their mind? The answer is likely to be 'no'. Therefore, the error in the Payable is unlikely to be a material one for the investor in making a decision on whether to invest.

Why is materiality important

- If financial statements contain a material misstatement they cannot show a true and fair view (as highlighted in the above worked example).
- Auditors therefore must design their audit procedures to reduce the risk of material misstatement to an acceptable level.
- The type of audit report issued will be determined by the presence and level of material error or misstatement (which we will see in a later chapter).

So the amount and nature of audit procedures is determined by:

- the level of risk
- materiality.

What is tolerable misstatement?

A monetary amount set by the auditor in respect of which the auditor seeks to obtain an appropriate level of assurance that the monetary amount set is not exceeded by the actual misstatement in the population.

[ISA 530]

In testing a particular population the auditor may be prepared to accept a different (usually lower) level of misstatement from the figure placed on materiality.

The reason for this is that some items can be determined with absolute accuracy, such as a bank account balance.

Conversely, there are other areas of the financial statements which are less absolute and involve an element of judgement in their calculation. For example, allowances for doubtful receivables. For such items, a higher level of error may be acceptable.

Exam focus

Materiality is quite a difficult concept to explain, so it is helpful to familiarise yourself with the quote from ISA 320 and to remember phrases like 'influence the economic decisions of users'.

- Materiality usually concerns the financial statements as a whole.
- Tolerable misstatement only concerns the population being tested.

It is preferable to use widely accepted terminology in the exam, rather than try to 're-phrase' something into your own words.

Remember, the examiner has confirmed that there will be marks available for 'rote learning' in the exam.

Materiality

chapter 8

Planning

In this chapter

- Purpose of planning.
- Stages of planning.
- Assessing risk.
- Materiality levels.
- Internal audit.
- Knowledge of the business (KOB).
- Design procedures.
- The planning memorandum.
- The planning meeting.

Purpose of planning

Planning enables the auditor to:

- focus on the important areas of the audit
- design procedures so that risks are addressed effectively
- ensure the work is carried out efficiently.

A cynic might say it's all about the FEE:

- **Focus**
- **Effective**
- **Efficient**

ISA 300 offers guidance on the area of audit planning.

Stages of planning

The purpose of audit work is to reduce the risk of the financial statements being materially misstated or, in other words, so that AR = an acceptable level. Therefore, the planning process must start with:

- assessing risk
- determining materiality.

Exam focus

Students should appreciate and recognise the difference in assessing risk and determining materiality for an existing client compared to the same task for a new audit client.

Then the auditor can:

- decide what evidence is needed
- design suitable audit procedures to obtain it.

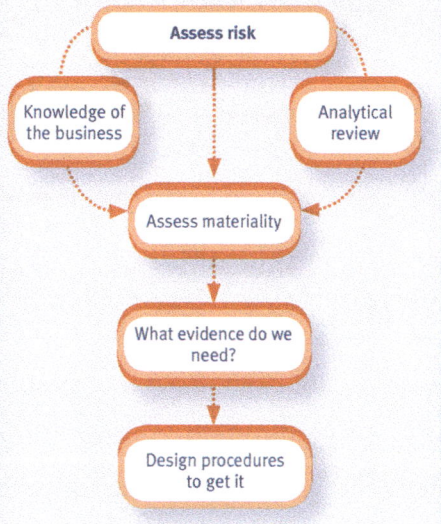

The planning cycle

Planning is virtually continuous. At the end of the previous audit:

- consider independence issues
- carry forward points affecting future audits.

Before the year end:

- organise specific procedures:
    - inventory count attendance
    - bank letter
    - receivables list for circularisation
    - tax planning.

Between the year end and the start of fieldwork:

- pick the audit team (this should result in the appropriate personnel, for an appropriate length of time)
- preliminary audit fee budget.

Planning

Before the start of fieldwork:

- risk assessment (e.g. low / medium / high)
- preliminary analytical review (e.g. use of analytical procedures, such as ratios, comparisons, variance analysis)
- determine materiality (use of judgement and previous knowledge/experience)
- determine audit approach (all audit should be risk based)
- determine sample sizes (should be representative)
- allocate tasks (all personnel should be clear about their role – good quality controls in the practice should ensure this)
- finalise budget (the fee must be agreed with the client, before commencement of the audit)
- determine deadlines (deadlines must be agreed with audit staff and the client).

The Planning Cycle

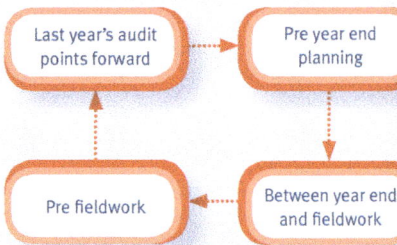

Assessing risk

The auditor should perform the following risk assessment procedures to obtain an understanding of the entity and its environment, including its internal control:

(a) enquiries of management and others within the entity (e.g. internal audit)

(b) analytical procedures (e.g. reasonableness checks), and

(c) observation and inspection.

[ISA 315]

Therefore, there are two sources of information for assessing risk:

- knowledge of the business (see below)
- analytical review.

Materiality levels

- Materiality is a matter of professional judgement, so firm quantitative guidance is rare.
- Many firms use the following as starting points:
  - 0.5 to 1% of revenue, or
  - 1 – 2% of gross assets, and
  - consider 5 – 10% or profit/loss before tax as a further indicator.
- For some industries – e.g. manufacturing, distribution, retail – the revenue basis will be most appropriate.
- For others – e.g. property, construction, banking – the assets basis will be better.

If you are still unsure about materiality, look back now at the previous chapter.

Planning

Internal audit

Definition of internal audit: an independent, objective assurance and consulting activity designed to add value and improve an organisation's operations.

The need for internal audit depends on:

- scale, diversity and complexity of activities
- number of employees
- cost/benefit considerations
- the desire of senior management to have assurance and advice on risk and control.

What do internal auditors do?

Knowledge of the business (KOB)

Key Point

The importance of the auditor's KOB is reflected by the fact that there is a whole ISA (ISA 315) dedicated to it.

What do you need to know about the client's business?

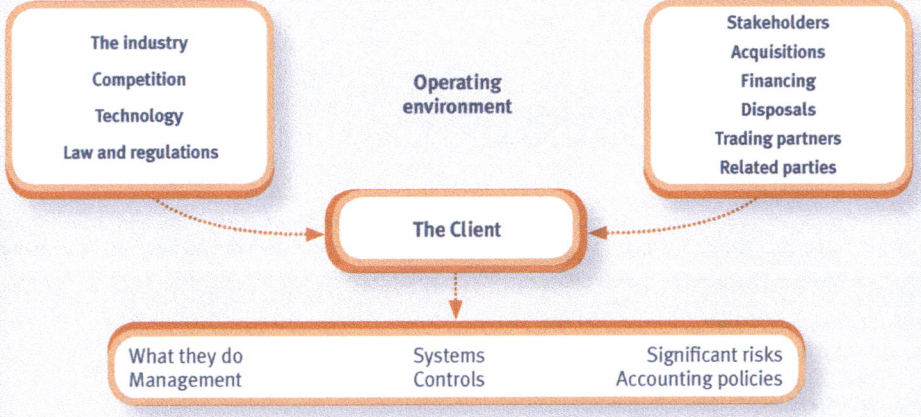

Operating environment

- The auditor should understand the impact and influence that the nature of the industry, laws and regulations, etc. have on the operating environment.

For example, if a new safety regulation were issued, the auditor must consider whether the business has taken steps to implement the change and ensure compliance with the new regulations.

Consider also the associated risk for non-compliance (perhaps loss of licence for the business?)

- The auditors should understand the impact and influence that the owners, providers of finance, related parties, etc. have on the operating environment.

For example, where there are related party transactions, the auditor must consider whether disclosures are in accordance with the relevant international accounting standard.

Inside the client itself:

- What it does.
- Management.
- Accounting policies.
- Significant risks.

By understanding the above factors, the auditor will be better positioned to assess the effectiveness and appropriateness of the following:

- Systems.
- Controls.

Definition

Significant risks are risks that require special audit consideration as they are likely to have a more material impact on the audit.

For example, if the newly appointed finance director comes from an organisation, whose audit report was subject to a modified opinion, the audit plan should take account of this fact and the plan should be modified accordingly.

Any list of significant risks in a business is not definitive, but sources of KOB should assist in identifying them.

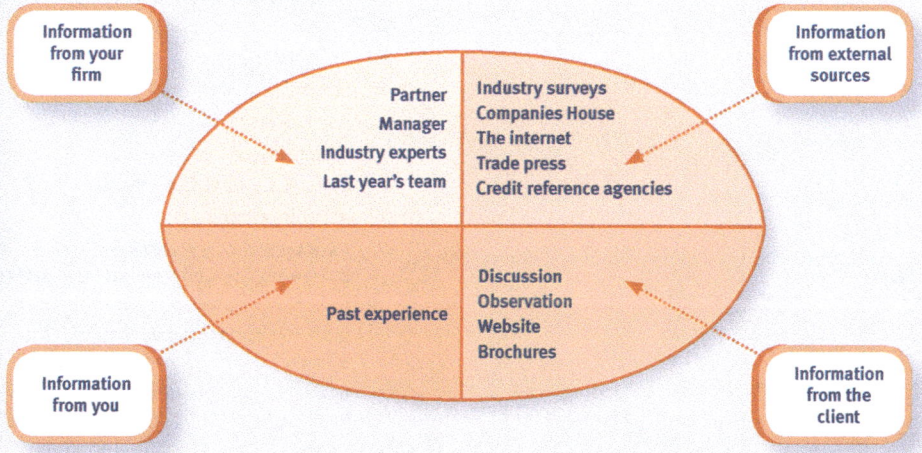

Planning

Design procedures

- Audit procedures are dealt with in detail in Chapter 10 Gathering evidence.
- Audit procedures should be targeted at identified risks (ISA 330).

The planning memorandum

Definition

A document that summarises the planning process.

The planning memorandum has the following contents:

- the audit team
- summary of KOB
- risk assessment
- materiality
- preliminary analytical review
- audit approach
- assessment of the auditor's independence and any potential threats to it
- audit fee budget (as agreed with the client)
- timetable (as agreed with the client and audit staff)
- partner approval.

The planning meeting

All the planning and KOB is useless unless communicated to those who need it.

Purpose of planning meeting:
- share information
- identify and discuss risks.

Participants
- all key members of the team
- including the partner
- not necessarily everyone (however, it is important to communicate to those not in attendance, so everyone understands their role).

At the meeting, pay particular attention to:
- susceptibility to fraud
- professional scepticism
- the susceptibility of the entity's financial statements to material misstatements.

Details of the meeting should be documented as documented details will form part of the audit file, which becomes audit evidence.

Exam focus

The bulleted lists should help you with questions about e.g. the purpose of planning, the contents of the planning memorandum, etc.

Ensure that you understand and remember the components and sources of KOB.

By understanding the client's business, the risk of arriving at an inappropriate opinion is reduced. The greater the auditor's KOB, the greater the potential to mitigate AR and therefore, the auditor's exposure to liability.

Planning

chapter

Systems and controls

In this chapter

- Understanding systems.
- Recording systems.
- Internal control.
- The control environment.
- Control activities.
- Revenue controls.
- Cash controls.
- Non-current assets controls.

Understanding systems

Purpose of systems:

- collect data
- summarise data
- produce financial statements.

Exam focus

For the purpose of the exam (unless instructed otherwise), the student should always assume the presence of computerised systems.

However, for the purpose of comparison and in order to facilitate understanding, we will consider manual and computerised systems in turn.

Manual systems

```
Substance of transaction
          ↓
       Invoice
          ↓
   Day book/journal
          ↓
   Posting voucher
       ↙       ↘
Sales/Purchases   Nominal ledger
    ledger             ↓
                   Trial balance
                       ↓
                    Accounts
```

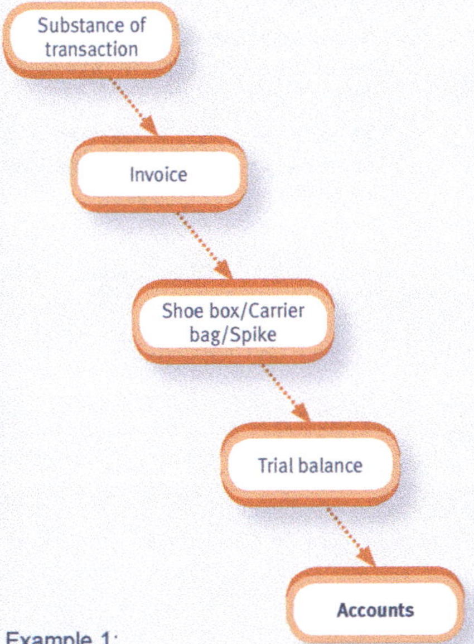

Chapter 9

Example 1: The classic view

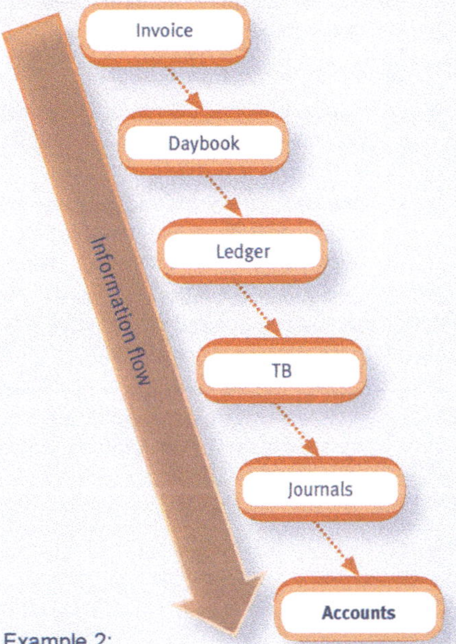

- Substance of transaction
- Invoice
- Shoe box/Carrier bag/Spike
- Trial balance
- **Accounts**

Example 2: The 'realistic' view

- Invoice
- Daybook
- Ledger
- TB
- Journals
- **Accounts**

Information flow

Systems and controls

Control implications of manual systems – disadvantages

Greater scope for error because:

- manual systems are operated by people (and are therefore susceptible to human error)
- information is transferred from document to document (therefore, there is potential for omission or transposition of data)
- more prone to simple errors and mistakes (e.g. sales invoice posted to the wrong customer account)
- controls can be more easily bypassed, ignored or overridden (particularly where there is no division of duties e.g. in small companies).

Control implications of manual systems – advantages

- Dealing with 'one off' transactions (e.g. item of capital expenditure may only occur once in a small company).
- Where the exercise of judgement is important (e.g. where a non-standard rate of discount is applicable).

Computerised systems

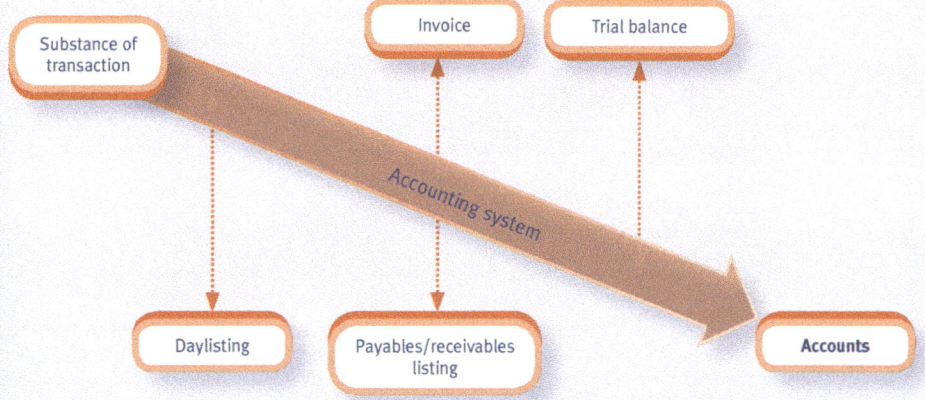

Systems and controls

System with on-line trading or linkages to suppliers' or customers' systems

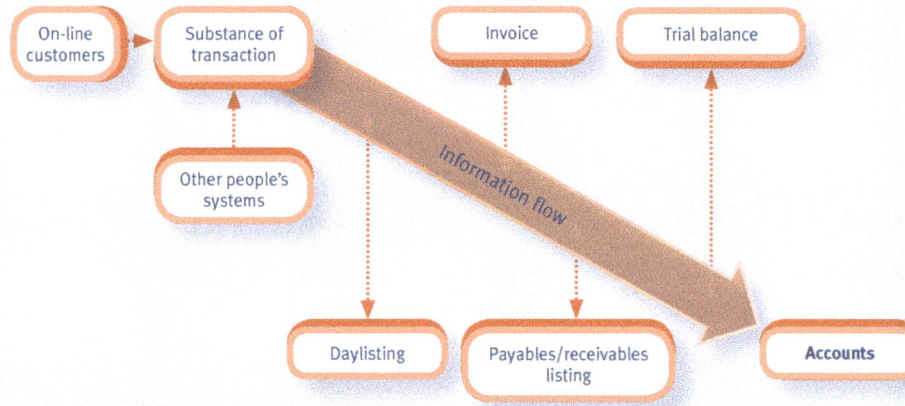

Control implications of computerised systems – advantages

- Consistent processing (data transferred uniformly to all relevant areas of the system).
- Accurate calculation (controls should prevent illogical posting, such as one-sided postings).
- Capacity to handle high volumes swiftly (far quicker than manual systems – this is the main advantage of a computerised system).

Control implications of computerised systems – disadvantages

- Little exercise of judgement
- Access to system = access to controls (whereas, it may not be appropriate for all staff to have unrestricted access to all areas of the system)
- Widespread impact of errors in:
  - installation
  - programming
  - override.

For example, a single error could have wide-reaching implications e.g. the incorrect input of the price of a supermarket product could significantly impact revenue figures, as every item of the same product will be incorrectly priced.

Controls over computer systems can be categorised as follows:

- **General controls:**
  - access restrictions – e.g. only senior management authorised to access the pricing system in a supermarket pricing system
  - passwords – e.g. files containing sensitive data such as payroll should be password protected, so that only Personnel / Human Resource dept can access the records.

- **Applications controls:**
  - built into system – e.g. one sided entries not permitted
  - arithmetic checks – e.g. presence of batch control totals
  - range checks – e.g. sales invoices must be within a given range of sequentially numbered sales invoices
  - validation.

Systems and controls

It is important to understand the system to:

- assess its reliability as a basis for preparing financial statements
- assess the effectiveness of controls
- design suitable audit procedures.

The auditor should obtain an understanding of the information system, including the related business processes, relevant to financial reporting.

[ISA 315]

Recording systems

The auditor must demonstrate an understanding of the client's systems, which can be done by recording the system. There are a number of methods the auditor can use to record the client's systems, which include:

1. Narrative notes – narrative description of systems and related controls
   - Easy and convenient.
   - Difficult for some to understand/use.
   - Can be long-winded.
   - Difficult to identify areas of controls which are omitted.

2. Flowcharts – diagrammatical version of systems and related controls (supplemented with narrative)

- Facilitates visibility of document flow to identify related procedures and checks.
- Helps to highlight weaknesses in controls.
- Assumes an understanding of symbols / terminology.

Also organisational charts and Internal Control Questionnaires (ICQs), but less common than 1 and 2.

Efficient recording for audit purposes starts at the end and records how the information got into the accounts.

Recording the system

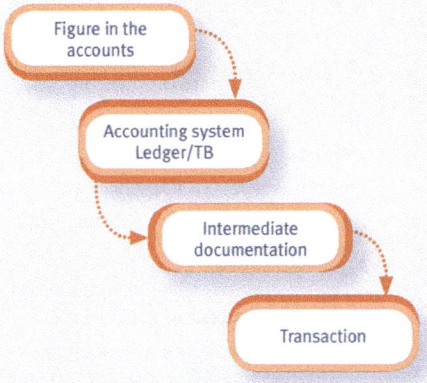

Whichever methodology is used for recording the client's systems, details are recorded and placed in the audit file.

Internal control

The purpose of controls

ISA 315 states that the purpose of internal control is to provide reasonable assurance about achieving the entity's objectives with regard to:

- reliability of financial reporting
- effectiveness and efficiency of operations
- compliance with applicable laws and regulations.

In terms of financial statement assertions (see later), the objective is to ensure:

- All valid transactions are recorded (Completeness, Cut-off).
- Only valid transactions are recorded (Occurrence, Existence, Rights and Obligations, Cut-off).
- Transactions are recorded accurately (Accuracy, Valuation).
- Transactions are allocated to the correct accounts (Classification, Allocation).

Internal control components

- Control environment – see below.
- Risk assessment – the client's own procedures and processes for assessing the risks it faces.
- Information system – effective or not?
- Control activities – see below.
- Monitoring – what does the client do to ensure its controls are effective?

[ISA 31

The control environment

Before embarking on any detailed audit testing, the auditor should assess the effectiveness of the client's control environment.

The following factors are indicative of a strong control environment:

- communication and enforcement of ethical values
- commitment to competence
- participation by those charged with governance
- management's philosophy and operating style
- organisational structure
- assignment of authority and responsibility
- human resource policies and practices.

[ISA 315]

The presence of these factors should indicate a reduction in the level of control risk (and therefore, audit risk).

Control activities

- Authorisation – e.g. payment approved by senior staff.
- Performance reviews – e.g. timely comparisons with budgets, targets, etc.
- Information processing (whether it is a good system and operated effectively).
- Physical controls – e.g. safes, locked doors, security, CCTV).
- Segregation of duties:
  - no one person responsible for all aspects of a transaction from start to finish
  - between who has custody of assets and who maintains the records of assets.

Exam focus

There are three areas which are examined regularly in terms of controls. Those relating to:

- revenue / receivables
- cash
- non-current assets

We will consider each in detail, but there are three aspects to the controls which should be understood:

Control objectives – this is the aim of putting a control in place (the reason a control exists)

Control procedures – this is the actual control which should be enforced / carried out (in order to meet the control objective)

Control tests – this is the test the auditor can carry out in order to see whether the control procedure is actually effective (to see if it is doing what it is designed to do).

Revenue controls

Objectives:
- Prompt recording of customer orders and sales invoices.
- Only those goods ordered are to be delivered / provided.
- Invoices and credit notes details should be checked for accuracy.
- Credit notes to be issued by authorised personnel only.
- Receivable balances should be monitored for slow / bad payers.

Procedures:
- Limits to be established for credit customers.
- Credit control dept to carry out monthly review of credit customers' balances.
- Credit control must evidence their review.
- Sales orders should be recorded, delivery notes issued and invoices raised and sent to customers.
- Invoices should be recorded promptly.
- Statements must be issued periodically detailing unpaid balances for credit customers.

Tests:
- Inspect invoices to ensure issued numerically.
- Perform computation of sales invoice and credit note details for accuracy.
- Inspect customer account records for evidence of credit control review.
- Observe despatch process.
- Inspect credit notes to ensure appropriately authorised.
- Enquire about policy for allowances for bad / doubtful receivables.
- Inspect irrecoverable receivables write offs for appropriate approval.
- Observe and inspect reconciliation of sales order to despatch note to sales invoice.

Cash controls

Objectives:
- To ensure monies due are received and recorded accurately.
- To ensure actual receipts and payments are recorded promptly and accurately.
- To ensure control over payments.

Procedures:
- Post is opened by responsible person and date stamped.
- Cash / cheque receipts are recorded immediately.
- Cash / cheque books are kept secure.
- Cash sales are recorded on pre-numbered invoices and receipts issued.
- Cash is reconciled to invoices and receipts.
- Cash is banked promptly.
- Cheque payments are signed by an authorised signatory.
- Cheques are not pre-signed
- Bank reconciliation carried out regularly say monthly.
- Petty cash is capped at, say, $200 and transactions must be documented on petty cash voucher.
- Petty cash tin should be locked up.

Tests:
- Observe mail opening procedure.
- Perform arithmetical checks on receipts
- Enquire whereabouts of petty cash tin.
- Observe cheque request and cheque payment procedures (for segregation).
- Inspect bank mandate to verify authorised personnel.
- Perform bank reconciliation.
- Inspect payment requests for appropriate approval and supporting documentation
- Inspect petty cash vouchers and calculate petty cash balance to float level, say $200.

Non-current assets controls

Objectives:
- Must be correctly recorded and kept safe.
- Acquisitions / disposals must be properly authorised.
- Acquisitions/ disposals should achieve best price.
- Appropriate rates of depreciation should be charged.

Procedures:
- Maintain a non-current assets register.
- Do periodic physical checks.
- Insure and maintain the non-current assets.
- Disposals and acquisitions to be authorised by directors.
- Depreciation rates are set by the Financial Controller.
- Disposal proceeds should be recorded and reconciled to non-current assets register.

Tests:
- Inspect board minutes for appropriate approval of acquisitions / disposals.
- Inspect non-current assets register.
- Inspect insurance policy documentation.
- Enquire about maintenance of non-current assets.
- Compute depreciation.
- Observe physical security controls.

Exam focus

The areas above are those which are examined most regularly, but other areas of control systems, which are also examined include:

- Purchases / Payables.
- Payroll.
- Inventory.

As practice, see if you can think of control objectives, control procedures and some audit tests of the controls relating to these other areas of business.

Systems and controls

chapter

10

Gathering evidence

In this chapter

- Audit evidence.
- Financial statement assertions.
- Procedures for gathering evidence.
- Reliability of evidence.
- Using experts.
- Representations.
- Sampling.
- Working papers.
- Audit files.

Audit evidence

Definition

Audit evidence is the information used by the auditor in arriving at the conclusions on which the audit opinion is based. Audit evidence includes the information contained in the accounting records underlying the financial statements and other information.

Audit evidence

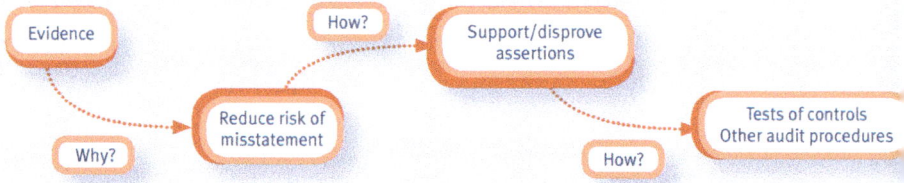

Why do we need evidence?

The auditor's instinct and judgement are very useful tools used throughout the audit process. However, these are not sufficient as a basis for the audit opinion.

As indicated in the definition above, the auditor must corroborate the opinion with facts gathered in the form of evidence.

Consider how difficult it would be for the auditor to defend an opinion without supporting evidence to substantiate the opinion given.

Financial statement assertions

Definition

Financial statement assertions are representations by management, explicit or otherwise, that are embodied in the financial statements.

Three categories of assertions:

- transactions and events
- account balances at the period end
- presentation and disclosure.

Transactions and events:

- Occurrence.
- Cut-off.
- Accuracy.
- Completeness.
- Classification.
- Presentation

Account balances at the period end:

- Existence.
- Rights and obligations.
- Completeness.
- Valuation and allocation.
- Presentation

Understanding assertions

Assertions are the assumptions that an item has been correctly included in the financial statements.

The auditor's role is to test the assertion. If it is correct, then that aspect of the financial statements represents a true and fair view.

Gathering evidence

Example

Assume that non-current assets valued in the statement of financial position include a motor vehicle. It is assumed by the user of the financial statements that the vehicle has been included correctly and in accordance with the appropriate accounting standards.

The task of the auditor is to carry out certain checks to gain evidence on whether the assumptions implied by its inclusion on the statement of financial position are reasonable, such as:

Does the vehicle actually exist?

Is the business the true owner?

Has the value been recorded correctly?

Has the appropriate methodology been applied for impairment?

Exam focus

If possible, remember the official headings above. However, it may be easier to remember these four 'key questions' which summarise what the assertions are really about:

- Should it be in the accounts at all?
- Is it included at the right value?
- Are there any more?
- Is it properly classified/disclosed?

Then apply these when the exam question asks you to devise suitable audit procedures

These questions and the official assertions fit together like this:

Audit assertions			
	Transactions and events	**Account balances at the period end**	**Presentation and disclosure**
Should it be in the accounts at all?	Occurrence, Cut-off	Existence, Rights and obligations	Occurrence, Rights and obligations
Is it included at the right value?	Accuracy	Valuation	Accuracy and valuation
Are there any more?	Completeness	Completeness	Completeness
Is it properly disclosed?	Classification	Allocation	Classification and understandability

Procedures for gathering evidence

Seven methods of gathering audit evidence according to ISA 500:

- inspection:
  - of records and documents
  - of tangible assets
- observation (of processes and procedures)
- enquiry (of knowledgeable persons)
- confirmation
- recalculation
- reperformance
- analytical procedures.

Reliability of evidence

Not all evidence is of equal quality.

ISA 500 summarises the relative reliability of evidence:

Audit evidence – the five generalisations	
This is better	This is worse
Independent external evidence	Internally generated evidence
Internal evidence subject to effective controls	Internal evidence not subject to such controls
Evidence obtained directly by the auditor	Evidence obtained indirectly or by inference
Documentary	Oral
Original documents	Photocopies or facsimiles

Using experts

Earlier in these notes, we alluded to the fact that the auditor may, at times, need to call on further expertise. For example, in order to corroborate assertions which are specialised or more complex.

Examples of areas where experts might be required are as follows:

- Valuation of complex inventories, such as oil reserves.
- Measuring costs, such as those on long-term contracts.
- Determining the validity of a provision, such as a provision for a damages claim against the company.
- Establishing the accuracy of the pension provision.

When considering the use of an expert, the auditor should consider the following factors:

- Are they competent?
- Are they objective?
- At what cost does their expertise come?
- Is the cost worth the benefit?

Conflict often arises in this area as the auditor may seek expert corroboration, but the cost will usually be borne by the client, who may not see the value in the use of such experts.

In order to resolve such issues, the auditor should first consider whether in-house expertise is available.

This is another area of the audit where sound judgement is required.

Representations

Representations are confirmations received by the auditor concerning items affecting the financial statements.

Representations are usually sought from:

- Management.
- Directors.
- Employees.

Representations can be:

- Written.
- Verbal / oral.

Using the rules of reliability, which of these do you think is more reliable as a form of evidence?

Answer: Written (documentary evidence).

Main representations required:

- Directors' responsibility for financial statements.
- No fraud or irregularities.
- Full disclosure to auditors.
- Related parties.
- Compliance with contractual obligations.
- Compliance with laws and regulations.
- Completeness.
- Fair values.
- No plans which will impact on values.

The most common method is the letter of representation:

- Representation letters are compulsory.
- Detailed provisions are set out in ISA 580.

Sampling

Earlier in these notes, we alluded to the fact that it is impractical for the auditor to test 100% of all transactions.

In order to reduce the amount of work the auditor carries out, we considered the fundamental principle of materiality.

Sampling is another means of reducing the amount of work carried out by the auditor.

Definition

Sampling is the application of audit procedures to less than 100% of items within an account balance or class of transactions such that all sampling units have a chance of selection.

This will enable the auditor to obtain and evaluate audit evidence about some characteristic of the items selected in order to form or assist in forming a conclusion concerning the population from which the sample is drawn.

Types of sampling

- Statistical
  - Random.
  - Systematic.
- Non-statistical
  - Haphazard/Judgemental.

Advantages of statistical sampling

- Representative of population.
- Results can be evaluated using probability theory.

Sample sizes

- The larger the sample, the lower the risk.
- Small samples provide minimal statistical assurance.

Directional testing

Whether you are testing for overstatement (existence/occurrence) or understatement (completeness) will determine where you select your sample from (the direction of the test).

Gathering evidence

Directional testing for overstatement

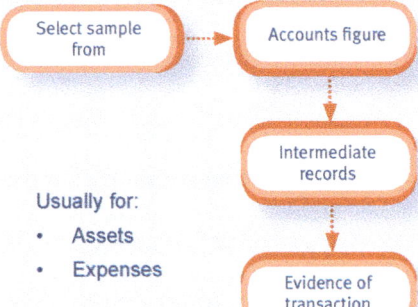

Usually for:
- Assets
- Expenses

Directional testing for understatement

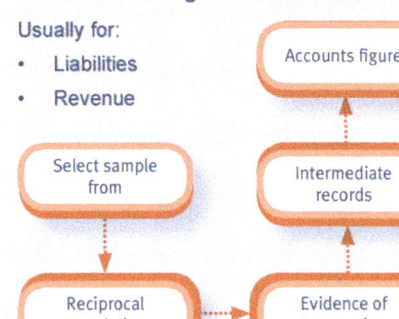

Usually for:
- Liabilities
- Revenue

Exam focus

In order for valid conclusions to be drawn in questions involving sampling, the sample **must be representative** of the population as a whole.

Working papers

General principles

- Audit opinions are based on evidence.
- If the auditor does not record audit work, there is no evidence.
- 'The unrecorded test never took place'.
- The reviewer needs to be able to understand what you did.

Working papers communicate:

- What you did.
- Why you did it.
- What your conclusions were.

Main contents

- Objective.
- Method.
- Results.
- Conclusions.

Working paper 'header' contents

- Client.
- Year end.
- Audit area/nature of work.
- Identity of person doing the work.
- Date work done.
- Identity of reviewer.
- Date of review.

File structure

- Accounts and completion.
- Review and finalisation.
- Planning.
- Audit areas – section by section.

Gathering evidence

File structure

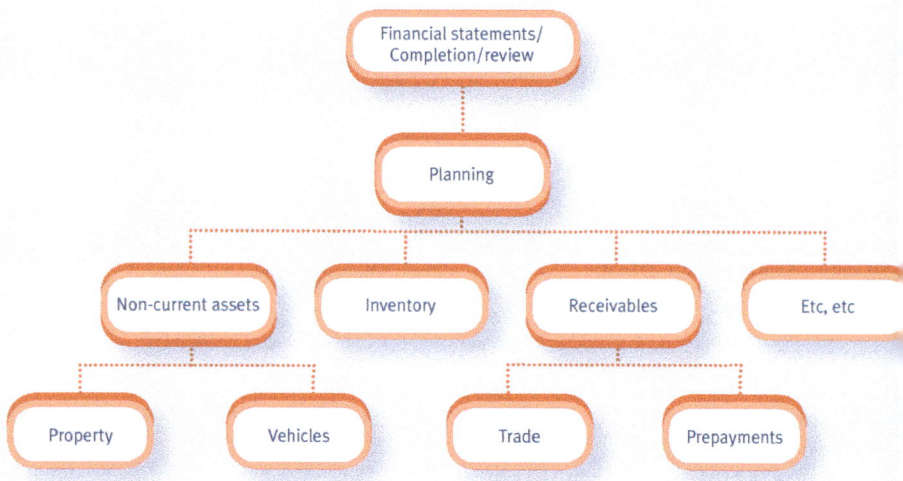

Section structure

- Lead schedule.
- Matters arising.
- Audit programme.
- Detailed working papers:
  - Sub-sections where appropriate.
  - All papers cross-referenced.

Section structure

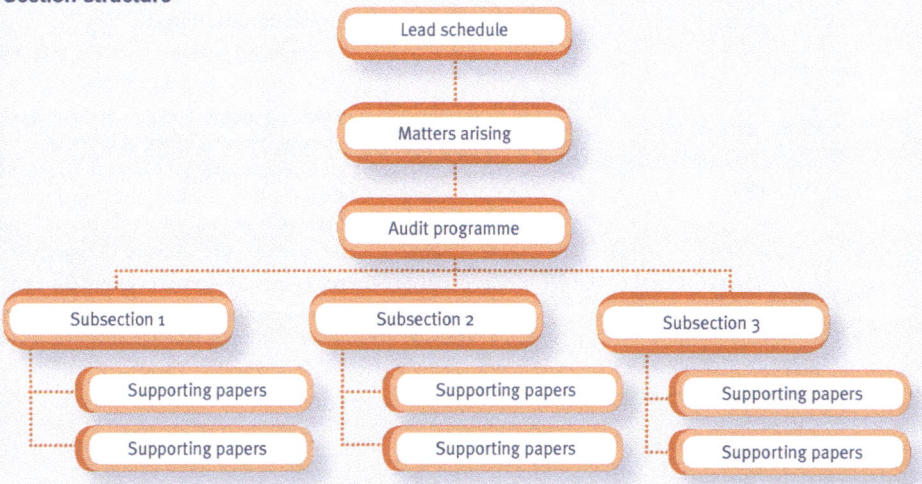

Gathering evidence

Audit files

This is where the working papers and all audit related documentation is kept.

There are two main files for each audit client:

1. Current file.
2. Permanent file.

Current file

- Papers and information needed for the current year's audit.
- Includes relevant background information:
  - KOB.
  - Systems.

Permanent file

- Standing data on client.
- Engagement letter.
- Background information.
  - KOB.
  - Systems.

- Information infrequently used:
  - Statutory information (Memorandum and Articles of Association).
  - Leases.
  - Directors' service contracts.

Changing nature of files

- Background information – KOB, systems etc – may be filed on either or both.
- Planning memoranda on current file usually include details of KOB, etc easily incorporated into word-processed document and edited and rolled forward from year to year which would previously have been held on the permanent file.
- All information on permanent file can be scanned in and carried about on a laptop, virtually incorporating it into the current file.

chapter 11

Audit verification work

In this chapter

- Audit programmes.
- Audit verification – Revenue.
- Audit verification – Purchases and expenses.
- Audit verification – Payroll.
- Audit verification – Tangible non-current assets.
- Audit verification – Investments.
- Audit verification – Receivables and prepayments.
- Audit verification – Bank and cash.
- Audit verification – Payables and accruals.
- Audit verification – Provisions.
- Audit verification – Inventory.
- Computers in auditing.

Audit programmes

The audit programme is a detailed plan which the auditor will follow in testing the components of the financial statements and its assertions.

Designing audit programmes

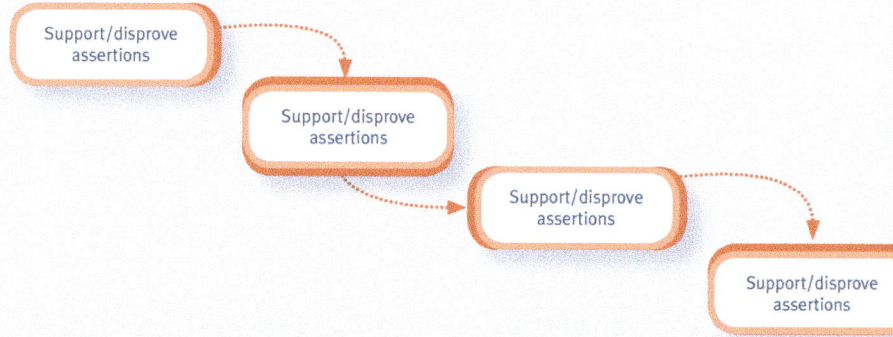

Common elements to audit programmes:

- assertions
- obtain or prepare lead schedule
- ascertain system
- test controls (if going to rely on them)
- analytical review
- record and evaluate errors
- report matters arising.

Audit verification – revenue

Assertion	Test
Occurrence	Check: • customer orders • despatch records • sales invoices • receipts.
Cut-off	Check despatch records and invoices either side of year end.
Accuracy	Check invoices and postings to accounting system.
Completeness	Check from despatch records, etc to invoices.
Classification	Check invoices and postings to accounting system.

Audit verification – purchases and expenses

Assertion	Test
Occurrence	Check: • orders • goods received records • purchase invoices.
Cut-off	Check goods received records and invoices either side of year end.
Accuracy	Check invoices and postings to accounting system.
Completeness	Often not tested explicitly. Assurance derived from occurrence testing on other areas.
Classification	Check invoices and postings to accounting system.

Audit verification – payroll

Occurrence	Check: • payslips • HR records • timesheets/clock cards • net pay payment run.
Cut-off	Check payroll dates and periods covered.
Accuracy	Check pay scales and operation of deductions for tax, social security and other deductions.
Completeness	Check for sub-contractors, other payments to individuals not on payroll.
Classification	Check postings to accounting system.

Audit verification – tangible non-current assets

Existence	Physical inspection.
	Inclusion on asset register.
Rights and obligations	Check:
	- title deeds (property)
	- registration documents (vehicles)
	- invoices (other assets).
Valuation and allocation	Check:
	- cost from invoices, title deeds, contracts, etc
	- valuation from surveyors' reports, etc
	- depreciation – reasonable rates, applied accurately
	- impairment
	- postings to accounting system inclusion on asset register.
Completeness	Often not tested explicitly.
	Assurance derived from existence and allocation testing on other areas.
	Inclusion on asset register.

Audit verification – investments

Existence	Check: • contract notes • share certificates, etc • portfolio reports from investment managers and custodians.
Rights and obligations	Check: • contract notes • share certificates, etc • portfolio reports from investment managers and custodians.
Valuation and allocation	Check: • contract notes • portfolio reports from investment managers and custodians • share valuation services • postings to accounting system.
Completeness	Assurance derived from existence and allocation testing on other areas Evidence of dividends and other related receipts tested elsewhere.

Audit verification – receivables and prepayments

Receivables

Existence	Confirm balances with customers. Check after date receipts.
Rights and obligations	Confirm balances with customers. Check after date receipts. Examine sales invoices.
Valuation and allocation	Confirm balances with customers. Check after date receipts. Review ageing. Review correspondence, etc. Postings to accounting system.
Completeness	Often not tested explicitly. Assurance usually derived from completeness testing of revenue.

Prepayments

Existence	Check to invoices, etc.
Rights and obligations	Check to invoices, etc.
Valuation and allocation	Check apportionment of invoices, etc. Postings to accounting system.
Completeness	Review expenses incurred close to year end. Compare with previous years.

Audit verification – bank and cash

Existence	Bank confirmation. Cash count.
Rights and obligations	Bank confirmation.
Valuation and allocation	Bank confirmation. Check bank reconciliation. Cash count. Check postings to accounting system.
Completeness	Bank confirmation. Cash count.

Audit verification – payables and accruals

Payables

Existence	Agree to suppliers' statements or invoices.
Rights and obligations	Agree to suppliers' statements or invoices.
Valuation and allocation	Agree to suppliers' statements or invoices. Check postings to accounting system.
Completeness	Check: • post year-end payments for inclusion • major suppliers during the year • significant payables in previous year(s).

Accruals

Existence	Agree to invoices, etc.
Rights and obligations	Agree to invoices, etc.
Valuation and allocation	Check apportionment of invoices etc. Check postings to accounting system.
Completeness	Check: • post year-end payments for inclusion • accruals in previous year(s) • 'expected' accruals: rent, utilities, etc • tax balances – company tax, payroll deductions, sales tax, etc.

Audit verification – provisions

Existence	Check past history for adequate but not excessive provisions.
Rights and obligations	Check terms of business for warranty provisions, etc. Significant contracts for warranties and indemnity provisions. Pension scheme terms and conditions.
Valuation and allocation	Check past history for adequate but not excessive provisions. Check postings to accounting system.
Completeness	Check terms of business for warranty provisions, etc. Significant contracts for warranties and indemnity provisions. Pension scheme terms and conditions. Check deferred tax calculations.

Audit verification – inventory

Existence	Attend inventory count.
	Carry out test counts from inventory listing to floor.
	Review perpetual inventory reports.
	Confirm with third party custodians.
	Review expert inventory checkers' reports.
		Valuation and allocation	Check:
			• invoices
			• costing records
			• stage of completion
			• evidence of:
			  – damage
			  – obsolescence
			• cost/NRV comparison
			• further costs to completion
			• postings to accounting system.

Rights and obligations	Inspect invoices. Check for reservation of title. Check for inventory held for third parties. Check cut-off.	**Completeness**	All locations? Everything counted? Test count from floor to inventory listing.

Computers in auditing

We mentioned earlier in these notes that students should assume the presence of computers for exam purposes.

Generally this assumption relates to the computer systems used by the client. However, the auditor also makes use of computers in the audit process.

For example, most auditors and in particular, fieldwork staff use a laptop to record audit work completed.

One particular development of importance to the auditor is the development of programmes designed to 'audit through' the client's computer systems.

This allows the auditor to verify the computer processing procedures of the client.

The programmes are known as:

Computer assisted audit techniques (CAATs)

Good for:

- high volume populations
- testing IT-based controls.

Two types:

- audit software
- test data.

Main disadvantages:

- cost
- live testing can be perilous (potential for loss/corruption of client data)!

Chapter 11

Computer-based audit packs and working papers

- Same features of audit programmes and working papers as traditional paper-based systems.
- More efficient cross-referencing and 'drill down' to underlying schedules.
- Blurs the distinction between current and permanent files.

Exam focus

You need to learn the theoretical lists on assertions (from the previous chapter) and audit procedures. Make sure you understand the relationship between the assertions, the procedures and the suggested tests, area by area. This will enable you to come up with suitable tests as required by individual questions, because these need to be tailored to the requirements of the client in the question.

Audit verification work

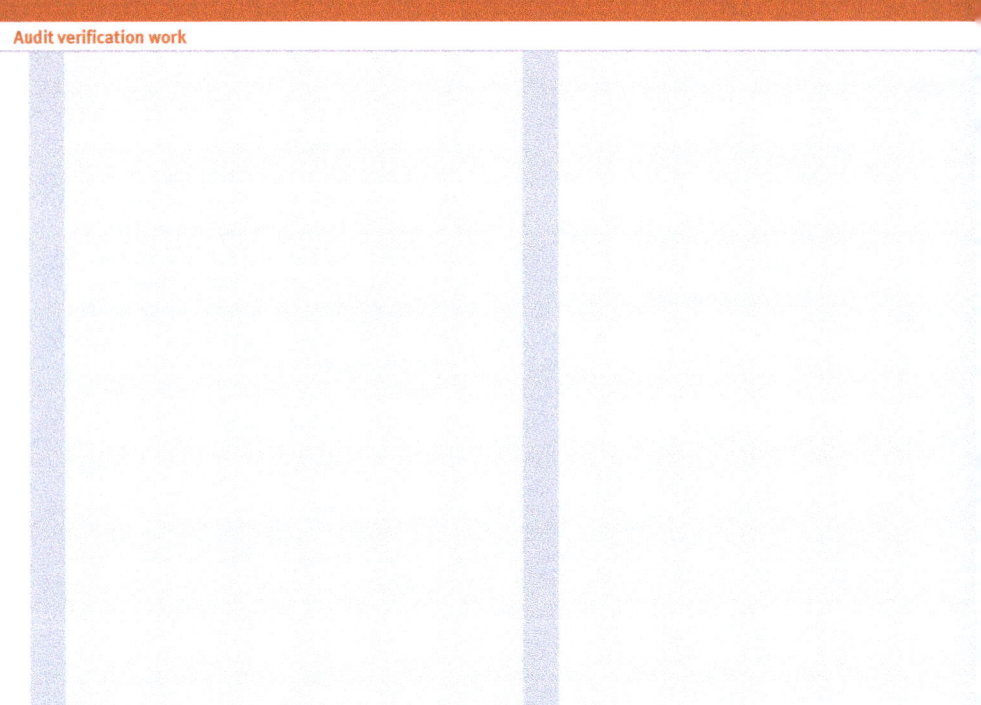

chapter 12

Final review

In this chapter

- Review.
- Completion memorandum.
- The management letter.
- Subsequent events review (ISA 560).
- Going concern (ISA 570).
- The representation letter.

Final review

Review

Upon completion of the audit testing, the engagement partner will carry out a final review of the audit file, prior to issuing an opinion on the true and fair view of the financial statements.

The key considerations at final review stage are reflected in the diagram below.

Completion

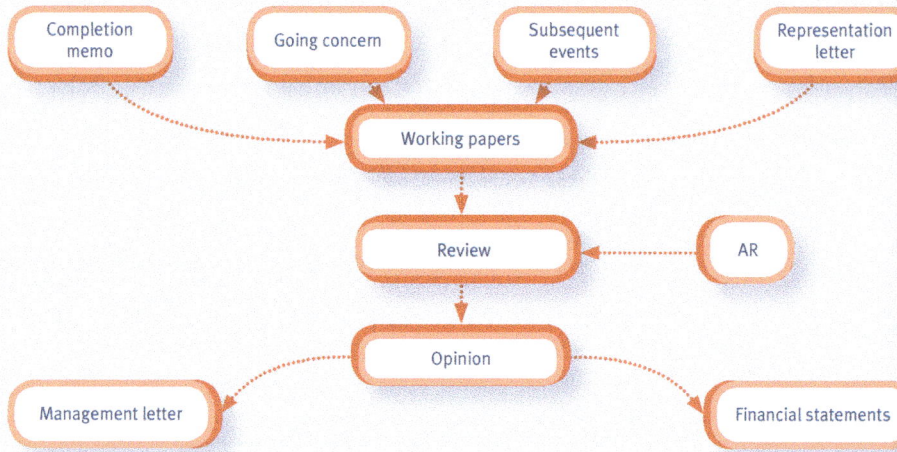

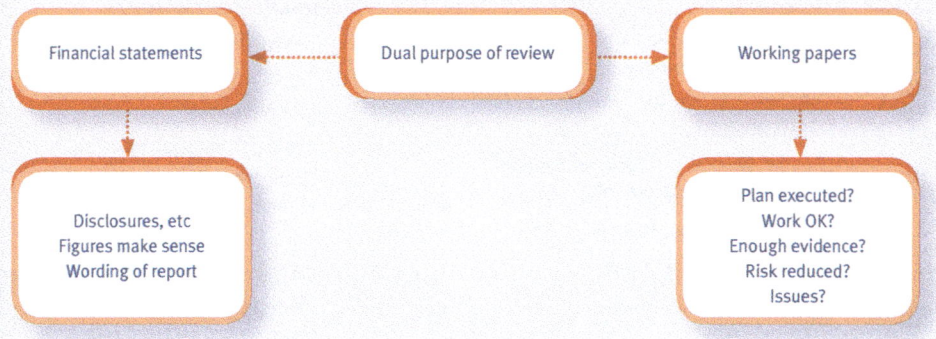

Purpose of review

- Quality control
  - Right work?
  - Enough work?
  - Risk reduced?
- Issues arising from the audit process
  - What are they? – e.g. was the client's ICS sufficient / effective?
  - Impact on opinion/report? – e.g. were issues resolved? If not, are they material?
  - Report to management? – Any unresolved, material issue should be reported to management.
  - Report to those charged with governance? – e.g. to the audit committee.

Final review

- Decisions
  - Opinion on the true and fair view of the financial statements.
  - Report (options are considered in the next chapter).
  - Other actions (management letter, reports to regulators, etc).

Different levels/types of review

- Senior review – aka 'hot review'
  - Detailed.
  - All papers.
- Manager review
  - Less detailed.
  - May/may not cover all papers (depends on experience of senior, firm's procedures, level of AR).
- Partner review
  - High-level review.
  - Focused on forming opinion.
- Independent partner review
  - Before the report is signed.
  - Objectivity?
  - Independence?
  - Justification for opinion reached?
  - Compulsory for listed and public interest clients.
- Final analytical review
  - Do the accounts really make sense - final check on ratios, etc.
  - Have all adjustments been made?
- Audit review dept
  - Carried out after the report is signed aka 'cold review'.
  - Some audit firms have a separate dept that is responsible for carrying out reviews to ensure that the firm's procedures are being followed.
  - Usually located in a different office from the one carrying out the audit.

Completion memorandum

The audit file should contain a completion memorandum, whose purpose is as follows:

Summarise everything to do with the audit in one accessible document.

- Highlight the issues.
- Facilitate review.
- Quality control.

Contents are as follows:

- Quick review of the key figures (derives from analytical review work).
- Deal with the key issues (derives from the matters arising schedules on each section).
- Summarise the audit approach section by section (derives from planning memorandum as amended by experience).
- Give an overall conclusion on the assignment.

The management letter

After the final review, but before the audit opinion report is issued, the auditor sends a report to management, whose main purpose is to:

- Draw management's attention to deficiencies in control uncovered during the audit.
- Recommend solutions.
- Not a substitute for modifying the audit report.

Contents

- Covering letter.
- Report itself.

The covering letter

- By-product of the audit.
- Limitations – does not necessarily cover all deficiencies which exist (focuses on material issues).
- Restrictions on use.
- Includes an acknowledgement of client' help and co-operation.

Format of report itself

- Nature of any deficiency – e.g. no controls over purchases.
- Implications – e.g. business's exposure to running out of inventory or excess inventories, also the need for detailed audit testing of purchase invoices and orders.
- Recommendations – e.g. dedicated authorised personnel only responsible f purchases.
- Columnar or paragraphs.

Subsequent events review (ISA 560)

Why are we interested in subsequent events?

- Adjusting events – events which tell us more about transactions during the year or balances at the year end.
- Non-adjusting events – other events relevant to users of the financial statements.

Auditor responsibilities relating to subsequent events

- Up to the date of the audit report, the auditor must watch out for subsequent events that might require adjustment or disclosure in the financial statements.
- After the date of the audit report, the auditor has no duty to actively search for subsequent events. However, if he does learn of subsequent events, he should discuss the matter with the directors and consider whether amended financial statements are necessary.

Audit procedures – for period up to signature of report

- Review relevant procedures set up by management.
- Read minutes of relevant meetings.
- Read interim financial statements and management accounts.
- Make enquiries of lawyers and other relevant advisers.
- Make enquiries of management.

Exam focus

A review of events arising after the end of the reporting period is a vital part of the final stages of the audit process and one which students are expected to be familiar with the importance of.

Going concern (ISA 570)

Why are we interested in 'going concern'?

- Financial statements assumed to be prepared on 'going concern' basis. This means for the foreseeable future.

Definition

'Foreseeable future' = for at least the next 12 months.

- Values of assets and liabilities may need to be revised if the going concern basis does not apply. For example:
  - non-current assets – are re-classified as current assets
  - inventory – may be written down / off
  - recievables – may be written down / off
  - long-term liabilities – are re-classified as current liabilities.

Audit procedures – for period up to signature of report

- Review relevant procedures set up by management – consider whether new controls have been implemented.
- Read minutes of relevant meetings – e. obtain board minutes from statutory file
- Read interim financial statements and management accounts – if available.
- Review cash flow forecasts and eviden of liquidity.
- Make enquiries of lawyers and other relevant advisers.
- Make enquiries of management.

The representation letter

- Representation letters are compulsory.
- Contents are set out in Chapter 10 Gathering evidence.
- Letter is sent from management to the auditors (not as some students have indicated in past exams).

Exam focus

Concentrate on the purpose of the items dealt with in this chapter – review, management letter, completion memorandum. If you understand what they're for, you'll probably remember how to do them.

Final review

chapter

13

Reporting

In this chapter

- Structure of the audit report.
- Types of report.
- Modified audit reports without modification: Emphasis of matter.
- Types of modification to the audit opinion.

Structure of the audit report

Reporting is seen by many to be the most important aspect of the audit process and one with which students must be familiar.

Exam focus

The format of the report (as indicated by the diagram below) is laid out by ISA 700 and should be known by students. In particular, the opinion section must be fully understood.

The audit report

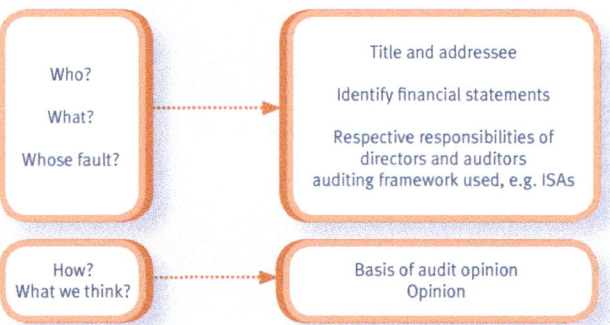

Types of report

There are three main categories of audit report:

- Unmodified – indicating that the FS represent a true and fair view, or are presented fairly.
- Modified audit reports without a modified opinion: Emphasis of matter.
- Modified – indicating that the FS (or at least, part of them) do not represent a true and fair view, or are not presented fairly (though there are a number of different types of modification.

Modified audit reports without modification: Emphasis of matter

These are used to draw the reader's attention to an item affecting the financial statements, but usually something not so serious as to give rise to a modification.

For example:

- Going concern issues.
- Where there is a significant uncertainty (e.g. pending lawsuit).
- Where the prior period comparatives have had to be restated in the current period.
- This does not constitute a modification, merely serves to highlight an important matter regarding the financial statements.

Types of modification to the audit opinion

There are two main bases for issuing a modified report. Either:

- the auditor identifies a material misstatement in the financial statements; or,
- the auditor is unable to obtain sufficient appropriate evidence.

What next?

The auditor's first aim when issuing a modified report is to determine the basis of modification. Having determined this, the auditor must establish whether the matter is **material** (of some concern) or **pervasive** (very serious / all encompassing).

Having determined the category of problem, the matrix below offers the solution to the type of audit opinion which the auditor must include in their report.

	Material misstatement	**Inability to obtain sufficient appropriate evidence**
Pervasive	Adverse opinion.	Disclaimer opinion.
Material but not pervasive	Qualified opinion true and fair except for the material misstatement.	Qualified opinion true and fair except for what might have been.

It should be apparent that the two most severe types of modified opinion are the '**disclaimer**' and '**adverse**' opinions.

In practice, the auditor should always attempt to resolve material misstatements and matters giving rise to the inability to obtain sufficient appropriate evidence with management and directors, before issuing a modified opinion report.

Reporting

Exam focus

Be familiar with the wording of audit reports as contained in your study text.

Remember the framework for modified opinions.

Index

Index

A

Advantages and disadvantages of an audit 30
Adverse opinion 117
Advocacy 4
Applications controls 65
Appointment of auditors 10
Assessing risk 51
Audit assertions 79
Audit evidence 76
Audit files 88
Audit manager 15
Auditor's duties 12
Auditor's responsibilities 26
Auditor's rights 13
Audit programmes 90
Audit report 114
Audit risk 35
Audit team 15

C

Cash controls 72
Completion memorandum 107
Computer assisted audit techniques (CAAT) 100
Computerised systems 63
Computers in auditing 100
Confidentiality 4
Control activities 70
Control environment 69
Control objectives 70
Control procedures 70
Control risk 36, 38
Control tests 70
Current file 88

D

Dealing with the client 23
Detection risk 36, 39
Directional testing 83
Disclaimer opinion 117

E

Emphasis of matter 115
Engagement considerations 20
Engagement letter 22
Engagement partner 15
Engagement process 21
Expectations gap 12
Experts 81

F

Familiarity 5
File structure 86
Financial statement assertions 68, 77
Fraud and error 28

G

General controls 65
Going concern (ISA 570) 110

I

Inherent risk 36
Integrity 3
Internal audit 52
Internal control 68
Internal control components 68
Internal v external audit 27
International Standards on Auditing 2
Intimidation 5

K

Knowledge of the business (kob) 53

L

Letter of representation 82

Index

M

Management letter 108
Management's responsibilities 26
Manual systems 62
Material but not pervasive 117
Materiality 42
Materiality levels 51
Modified audit reports 115

N

Non-current assets controls 73

O

Objective of the audit 31
Objectivity 3

P

Performance materiality 43
Permanent file 88
Pervasive 117
Planning 48
Planning cycle 49
Planning meeting 57
Planning memorandum 56
Procedures for gathering evidence 80
Professional behaviour 4
Professional competence and due care 3

Q

Qualified opinion 117
Quality control 17

R

Reasonable assurance 31
Reason for the audit 30
Recognised Supervisory Body (RSB) 10
Recording systems 66
Reliability of evidence 80
Representation letter 111
Representations 82
Responsible individuals (RIs) 10

Revenue controls 71
Review 104
Rights and duties 14
Risk 32

S

Sampling 83
Self-interest 4
Self-review 4
Subsequent events review (ISA 560) 109
Systems 60

T

The ACCA code 3
The engagement process 21
The importance of risk 34
The law 6
Tolerable misstatement 45
Types of report 115

W

Working papers 85

Index